NOTE TO PARENTS

Although every magic trick in this book has been kid-tested, and can, with practice, be easily performed by most children, some tricks are more difficult than others and may require your supervision. Please read every trick before allowing your child to do it. The RGA Publishing Group and SMITHMARK Publishers will not be held responsible for any injury that occurs during the practice or performance of a trick.

An RGA Book

HOPPIN' MAGIC

My First
Kitchen Kaper
MAGIC
TRICKS

Written by Stephanie Johnson

Illustrated by Kerry Manwaring

SMITHMARK

Cereal Box Prizes

What You'll Need:

- A box of cereal
- 2 identical cereal bowls
- A piece of cardboard
- A ruler
- Small hard candies
- A small colored scarf
- A bow tie
- Scissors
- A marker

Getting Ready:

1. First, you'll need to make a "Teddy Card," which you'll use to cover the prizes in your cereal bowl.

2. Draw a teddy bear head on the cardboard. This head should be ⅛ inc smaller all around than the diameter the bowl. (Measure from the tips of th ears to the chin, and from side to side

3. Cut out the teddy bear head. Cut out holes for the eyes so that you can use them as finger holes to pick up the card. Test the card by seeing if it fits snugly in the bowl while leaving enough space beneath it to hide your prizes. Trim off more around the edges if it won't fit.

4. Put the candies, scarf, and tie into one of the bowls and cover them with the Teddy Card. Now you're ready!

Doing the Trick:

1. Set the box of cereal and the two bowls on your show table. *Do not let your audience see the Teddy Card.* Say, "Here are two ordinary cereal bowls."

2. Pour some cereal into the empty bowl. Say, "The problem I have every morning is that I can put more into this bowl [point to the Teddy Card bowl] than I can into this bowl [point to the empty bowl with the cereal in it]."

3. Pick up the Teddy Card bowl, turn it upside down, and place it on top of the other bowl of cereal.

4. Pick up the bowls together and turn them upside down so that the cereal bowl is now on top of the Teddy Card bowl. Set the bowls on the table.

5. Take off the top bowl. Point to the Teddy Card bowl and say, "This bowl holds much more cereal. And it gives me prizes, too!" Brush some of the cereal off the Teddy Card, and use the finger holes to pull it out of the bowl. Hold it up and give it to a member of the audience. Pick out each of the gifts and give them to different audience members.

Water Colors

BLIPPITY, BLOPPITY, BLINK! MAKE THE WATER PINK!

Amaze your friends by turning a pitcher of clear water into red, blue, and purple.

What You'll Need:

- A blue plastic cup
- A red plastic cup
- A clear glass pitcher of water
- Tempera paint or food coloring (the same colors as the cups)
- A spoon
- A paintbrush

Getting Ready:

1. Paint the inside bottom of the cups with the paint or food coloring. Paint the blue cup blue and the red cup re Let the paint dry overnight.

2. Put the spoon in your pocket.

Doing the Trick:

1. First set the cups and pitcher on your show table and say, "I have here an ordinary pitcher of water and two magic cups." Hold the cups up to show your audience that they are empty. They will not notice the dry paint.

2. Say, "I will now pour some water into each of the cups." Fill each cup half full of water.

3. Take the spoon from your pocket and say, "I will now stir my magic spoon in the clear water and turn it into colored water."

4. Stir the water in the red cup first, scraping the spoon on the bottom of the cup to mix in the paint. Say, "Blibbity, blobbity, blink. Make the water pink!"

5. Set the spoon down on the table and pour the water from the red cup back into the pitcher. The water will turn pink.

6. Now stir the water in the blue cup—don't forget to scrape the paint off the bottom of the cup. Tell your audience to watch the pitcher carefully. Ask them, "What color do you think the water will be?" Everyone will say, "Blue."

7. Pour the water from the blue cup into the pitcher. Everyone will be surprised to see the water turn purple!

It's in the Bag

What You'll Need:

- A large paper bag with the edges rolled down
- 2 paper or Styrofoam cups of the same size and color
- A small pitcher of milk, water, or fruit drink
- Scissors

Getting Ready:

1. Cut the bottom off one of the cups. Cut the rim off the other cup.

2. Stack the bottomless cup inside the rimless cup. You now have a "doubl[e] cup" that looks like one cup. Before performing this trick, practice your pouring skills!

Doing the Trick:

1. Put the double cup on your show table. Show the audience that the bag is empty. Say, "This is my magic bag. It won't get wet even when I pour liquid into it."

2. Put the double cup into the bag so th[at] it is standing up on the bottom of the bag. Wave your wand over the bag and say, "Magic wand, turn this bag into a magic waterproof bag!"

3. Reach into the bag and take out the bottomless cup, leaving the rimless cup in the bag. *Make sure your audience does not see the hole in the bottom of the cup.* Set the cup on the table.

4. Pick up the pitcher and carefully pour the liquid into the bag. Make sure you pour it into the rimless cup. The audience will think that you are pouring the liquid right into the bag. As you are pouring, say, "This could make quite a mess in an ordinary bag."

5. When the rimless cup is about two-thirds full, stop pouring. Pick up the bottomless cup and say, "I will now dip my cup into the bag filled with liquid." Slowly insert the bottomless cup into the rimless cup to create a double cup once again.

6. Holding the double cup with both hands, lift it out of the bag and put it on the table.

7. Pick up the bag and show the inside to your audience. Say, "As you can see, my magic bag is nice and dry!"

Good Eggs, Bad Eggs

The "yolk" is on your audience members as you magically balance three eggs on end before their very eyes!

What You'll Need:

♦ 3 large raw eggs
♦ A patterned tablecloth
♦ 3 tablespoons of salt

Getting Ready:

1. At the front edge of your show table, place 3 tablespoons of salt in a row. Place the piles about 1 inch apart.

2. Carefully lay the tablecloth over the table so you don't disturb the piles. Make sure the piles cannot be seen by your audience.

Doing the Trick:

1. Show your audience the three eggs. Say, "I have here three ordinary eggs."

Ask for a volunteer to help you. Have him or her try to balance each egg on its end. The volunteer won't be able to do it.

When your volunteer has given up, say, "I will now use my magic wand to change these plain eggs into balancing eggs." Wave your wand over the eggs and say, "Abracadabra, ziggity zend! Make these eggs balance on end!"

Pick up one of the eggs and set it on its end on one of the piles hidden under the tablecloth. The salt will hold the egg in place. Proclaim, "One!" as you do this. Repeat with the second egg and say, "Two!" Do the same with the last egg and say, "Three!"

Mind-Reading Banana

Here's an "a-peel-ing" trick that will keep your friends and family guessing!

What You'll Need:

- A banana with a few dark spots on its peel
- A long needle or stick pin
- Up to 9 small pieces of paper
- A pencil
- A paper bag with the edges rolled down

Getting Ready:

1. Using the pencil, mark two very lig lines on the banana to divide it into three equal pieces.

2. Poke the needle into the banana where you made the first line. Move the needle left and right. This will cut the banana without tearing the peel.

3. Now poke the needle into the banana again, this time on the opposite side from where you poked it in step 2. Move the needle left and right. Repeat steps 2 and 3 with the second line.

Doing the Trick:

1. Set the banana, pencil, papers, and paper bag on your table. Hold up the banana and say, "I have here an ordinary banana. I will magically transform it into a mind-reading banana."

2. Take the pencil in your hand. Ask the audience to call out numbers between one and nine. Pretend to write each number on a piece of paper as it is called out—but really write the number 3 on all the pieces of paper, then drop them quickly into the bag. *Make sure the number 3 has been called out before going to the next step.*

3. Ask for a volunteer from the audience. Hold the bag high in the air and have the volunteer draw a piece of paper from the hat and read the number out loud. It will be 3.

4. Put the bag down. Wave your magic wand over the banana and say, "Hocus pocus, worlds of wonder! Great banana, tell the number!"

5. Now have the volunteer peel the banana. What will the volunteer find? The banana will be magically cut into three pieces!

Disappearing Water

MAGIC, MAGIC FAR AND NEAR, MAKE THE WATER DISAPPEAR!

What You'll Need:

- A dark or opaque beach pail with a handle (metal works better than plastic)
- A large super-absorbent sponge
- A pitcher of water
- Water-resistant glue
- Scissors

Getting Ready:

1. Cut the sponge to fit tightly into the bottom of the pail.

2. Glue the sponge into the bottom of th pail and let it dry overnight.

Doing the Trick:

1. Set the pail and the pitcher of water on your show table. *Make sure the audience does not see the sponge in the pail.* Say, "I have here an ordinary beach pail and a pitcher of ordinary water. I will now pour some water into the pail."

Pick up the pitcher and slowly pour a small amount of water onto the sponge in the pail. Unknown to your audience, the sponge will soak up the water.

Wave your wand over the pail and say, "Magic, magic far and near, make the water disappear!"

4. Lift the pail by the handle and hold it by your side. Swing your arm forward, then backward, then forward again in a big circle, like a Ferris wheel. Be careful not to hit anyone!

5. After making about four or five circles, stop swinging and put the pail back on the table. Ask if anyone has ever seen a pail of water swung like that without any water spilling out.

When someone in the audience says "Yes," do something unexpected— pick up the pail by its sides and turn it over your head! Then ask if anyone has ever seen a pail of water held like *this* before!

Magic Dust on Ice

What You'll Need:

- ☆ A clear glass bowl half filled with cold water
- ★ An ice cube
- ☆ A 12-inch piece of yarn or string (waxed or plastic-coated string will not work)
- ☆ A teaspoon of salt in a small "magic pouch" (or small container that can be hidden in your pocket)

Getting Ready:

1. Tie a loop at one end of the string. The loop should be big enough to fit snugly around the ice cube.

Doing the Trick:

1. Place the bowl of water in front of you on your show table. Drop the ice cube into the bowl. The cube will float.

2. Ask a volunteer to come onstage. Give the volunteer the string and ask him or her to lift the ice cube out of the water using only the string. The volunteer will try to loop the string around the cube but will not be able to do it.

3. When the volunteer has given up, take the string back and thank him or her for trying. Say, "My volunteer was unable to lift the cube from the water, but I, with the help of my magic dust, will be able to lift the cube with ease."

4. Dip the looped end of the string into the water until it is soaked.

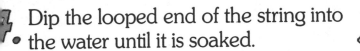

5. Lay the loop on top of the ice cube. Hold the other end of the string in your hand, or lay it carefully over the edge of the bowl.

6. Say, "I will now sprinkle magic dust over the string." Open your magic pouch and sprinkle a lot of the "dust" onto the cube where the string is laying.

7. Wave your wand over the bowl and say, "Hocus pocus, magic dust, do your magic work for us. Hocus pocus, magic string, work your magic, do your thing!"

8. Slowly lift up the string, and the cube will stay attached to it! (The salt makes the string freeze onto the ice cube!)

Quick Freeze

OOH! YOU MAY NEED YOUR MITTENS AND SCARF FOR THIS COOL TRICK!

Learn how to turn a little bit of water into an ice cube in just a few seconds!

What You'll Need:

- A dark colored plastic cup
- An ice cube   Scissors
- A super-absorbent sponge
- Water-resistant glue
- A pitcher of water

Getting Ready:

1. Cut the sponge so that it will fit into the bottom of the cup.

2. Glue the sponge into the bottom of the cup and let it dry overnight.

3. Just before you do the trick, set the ice cube on top of the sponge in the cup.

Doing the Trick:

1. Set the cup in front of you on your show table. *Don't let anyone see the sponge or the ice cube inside the cup.*

2. Say, "I will now pour some water into this ordinary plastic cup." Pour a little water into the cup. The sponge will absorb the water.

3. Wave your magic wand over the cup and say, "Magic Merlin, bright and bold, make the water hard and cold!"

4. Pick up the cup and turn it upside down over your show table. The ice cube will fall out, but the water won't!

How Dry I Am

Water is poured into a cup containing a handkerchief—but not a drop gets on the handkerchief. It's magic!

What You'll Need:

◆ 2 large 8- or 12-ounce cups
◆ A small 4- or 6-ounce cup
◆ Water-resistant glue
◆ A small pitcher of water
◆ A small handkerchief

Getting Ready:

1. Glue the small cup into the center of one of the big cups. Let the glue dry overnight.

2. Fill the other large cup one-third full of water.

3. Put the handkerchief in your pocket.

Doing the Trick:

1. Set the cups on the show table. *Do not let the audience see the small cup inside the big cup.* Say, "Here are two ordinary paper cups. One is filled with water, and the other one is empty."

2. Pull the handkerchief out of your pocket and show it to the audience. Say, "This is a magic handkerchief. Watch closely."

3. Stuff the handkerchief into the small paper cup that is glued into the big cup. *Don't let your audience see the small cup!*

4. Pick up the cup of water and say, "I will now pour water from this cup into the other cup." Slowly pour the water into the big cup, *making sure you do not get any in the small cup that holds the handkerchief.*

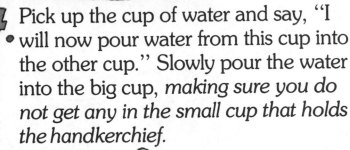

5. Now turn the first cup over to show that there is no water left in it. Then turn it right side up and set it on the table.

6. Say, "I will now pour the water from the second cup back into the first cup." Pick up the cup and pour the water back into the first cup, *but be careful not to get the handkerchief wet!*

7. When you've finished pouring, put the cup down. Say, "And as you will see, there isn't a drop of water on my magic handkerchief!" Reach into the cup and pull out the dry handkerchief!

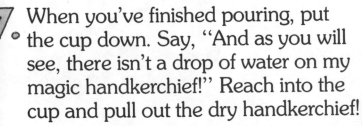

The Paper Plate Psychic

Learn how to be a mind reader with this simple trick!

What You'll Need:

- 3 paper plates (the kind with ribbed edges works best)
- Red, green, and blue markers or poster paints
- A pencil
- A paintbrush

Getting Ready:

1. Color the front side of one plate red. Then color the front of the second plate green and the front of the third one blue. If you use paint, let it dry overnight.

2. On the front edge of each plate, make a small pencil mark. Try to hide the mark in a crease if you can.

Doing the Trick:

1. Show the colored plates to your audience and say, "These are three ordinary paper plates that have been colored."

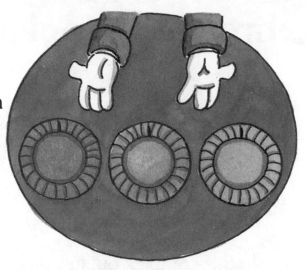

2. Place the plates color side up in a row on your show table. *Make sure you line up all the pencil marks on one side.*

3. Now ask for a volunteer. Say, "I am going to turn around, and when I do, I want you to choose one plate and show the colored plate to the audience. Then put the plate back on the table exactly where it was, and concentrate hard on the color you chose." Turn your back to the audience while the volunteer chooses a plate.

4. When the volunteer is done, turn around. Pretend to concentrate very hard on the paper plates. Look for the one pencil mark that is not lined up with the others. The plate that has this mark is the one that the volunteer chose.

5. Pick up the plate and announce, "This is the one you picked." You'll be right!

Shredded Napkin

In this complex but fun trick, you can magically put a torn napkin back together again!

What You'll Need:

◄ Small paper napkins (2 for the trick, and more with which to practice)

Getting Ready:

1. Crumple up one of the napkins into a ball. Be careful not to tear it. Make a fist to hide the ball in the palm of you left hand.

2. Practice this trick several times before you perform it. It will be hard at first t keep the napkin completely hidden ir your hand.

Doing the Trick:

1. Hiding the crumpled napkin in your left hand, set the pile of napkins on your show table. Say, "I have here a pile of ordinary paper napkins."

Take one napkin from the pile with your right hand. Hold one corner of the napkin with the thumb and index finger of your right hand, and the other corner with the thumb and index finger of your left hand, still keeping the crumpled napkin hidden. Tear the napkin in half.

3. Crumple the two halves together into a ball and hold the crumpled halves with the fingers of your right hand.

With your left hand, wave your magic wand over the two halves and say, "Alakazoo, alakazam! Make this napkin whole again!"

5. Set down your wand. Put the torn napkin into your left hand, making sure that you put it under the crumpled whole napkin.

Keeping the torn napkin hidden in your palm, work the crumpled whole napkin to the fingertips of your left hand while you say some more magic words.

7. Now reach across with your right hand and unfold the crumpled whole napkin!

Salt into Pepper

In this trick, amaze your friends and family by turning salt into pepper!

What You'll Need:

- ★ A clear glass saltshaker with a screw-on top
- ★ A white paper napkin
- ☆ Salt and pepper

Getting Ready:

1. Fill the saltshaker with salt. Don't put the cap on yet!

2. Unfold the napkin and lay it over the top of the shaker. Put a small pile of pepper on the napkin over the mouth of the shaker.

3. Screw on the cap. Be careful not to let any pepper fall into the shaker!

4. Tear off the rest of the napkin. Make sure no part of the napkin is sticking out from under the cap.

Doing the Trick:

1. Set the shaker on your show table. Say, "I have here an ordinary saltshaker filled with ordinary salt. Can you all see the salt?" Your audience will answer yes.

2. Say, "I will now change the salt to pepper." Wave your wand over the shaker and say, "Shazam!"

3. Ask for a volunteer. Tell the volunteer to hold out his or her hand. Pick up the saltshaker and shake it into the volunteer's hand. Pepper will come out!